DIVINE WHISPERS
[UNLEASH]

DIVINE WHISPERS [UNLEASH]

LETTING GO OF WHAT IS BEHIND TO REACH OUT FOR WHAT IS AHEAD

DR SUMBO NDI

CLARIFY TO SUCCEED PRESS

DIVINE WHISPERS: UNLEASH (VOLUME 1)
Copyright © 2021 SUMBO NDI

ISBN: 9780645275100 (Print version)
ISBN: 9780645275117 (ePub Edition)

Editor: Nan Berrett (Word Solutions)
Interior illustration: Pixabay
Publisher: CLARIFY TO SUCCEED PRESS (Contact: ctspress@sumbondi.com.au)

First Printing, 2021

Dedication

I dedicate this book of poems and return all the glory to almighty God- Father, Son and Holy spirit for divine inspiration and nudging to write.

To my children. I pray your faith, hope, love and trust in God is deepened by the text on these pages.

To my husband, my best friend, challenger and cheerleader. I pray you are enriched and inspired as you have been for me every step of the way.

To my parents, you are one of a kind. Mum, I pray you are blessed and touched. Dad, I know you are smiling in heaven.

To all my family and friends. I pray God will touch your hearts as you have touched mine in profound ways.

To you precious person reading the book. I pray you are inspired and encouraged; and get the revelation that God has been with you and whispering to you all along.

Contents

Dedication   v
Preface   xi

INTRODUCTION   1

UNDERSTAND THERE IS MORE FOR YOU   5

1 QUEEN INSIDE OF YOU   6
2 BEAUTIFUL   10
3 O CHILD   13
4 ACCEPTED   16
5 BLESSED   19
6 WORTHY   22
7 YOU CALL ME BY NAME   25

NEVER ALLOW THE PAST OR PRESENT RESTRAIN YOU 29

8 GOODBYE YESTERDAY   30

9 SCAR 33

10 KEEP MOVING 36

11 IN THE END 39

12 COURAGEOUS HEART 42

13 THE STORY I TELL MYSELF 45

14 A DATE WITH MY FUTURE 48

LET GOD BE YOUR STRENGTH **51**

15 STILL ABIDE 52

16 I KNOW 55

17 WHY 58

18 FOREVER SURE 61

19 WAIT 64

20 JOY 67

21 UNSTOPPABLE 70

ELIMINATE FEAR FROM YOUR LIFE **73**

22 PERFECT LOVE 74

23 WEEP NOT 77

24 I SEE 80

25 I WONDER 83

26 REST 86

27 I RUN TO YOU 89

28 YOU ARE   92

ALIGN YOUR WILL TO GOD'S WILL   95

29 IN YOU ALONE   96

30 WHO AM I WITHOUT YOU   99

31 THE MAKING OF A VESSEL   102

32 I RUN MY RACE   105

33 TIME   108

34 ONLY YOU   111

35 FOR ME   114

SET YOUR EYES ON THINGS ABOVE   117

36 HIGHER THAN I   118

37 FIRE IN MY SOUL   121

38 MORE THAN ENOUGH   124

39 SMELL THE ROSES   127

40 ETERNITY   130

41 WHEN I DON'T KNOW   133

42 LIGHT AND DARKNESS   136

43 I GO WITH YOU   139

HOLD ON TO THE WORD OF GOD   143

44 STAND AGAINST   144

45 READY   147

46 I WILL ARISE   150

47 WHISPER   154

48 THE MOMENT   157

49 COME FORTH   160

50 ROAR   163

UNLEASH   **167**

Sample: Volume 2   170
Prayer Of Salvation   174
About The Author   175
Image Credit   176

Preface

Dear reader, congratulations for joining me on this journey of exploring Divine Whispers. Let your heart and mind be open as you read and take in the meaning, wisdom and insight that will come up for you.

Divine whispers is a collection of uplifting and inspirational poems, thoughts and prayers written over a period of time. They were written during moments of deep introspection, inspiration and contemplation about many facets and aspects of life and human experience. Many were written from sensing a burden or emotions which had no external circumstances creating them. Over time, I came to understand the impulse and learnt to follow the instruction to capture and write down what the experience was communicating.

I express profound gratitude to everyone who inspired me and offered feedback along the way. Thank you very much Nan Berrett for editing and for your feedback. A special thank you to my family for allowing me the time and space for contemplation and writing. Most importantly, I thank God for the grace and wisdom that has made this possible.

UNLEASH

VOLUME 1

INTRODUCTION

The poems and thoughts captured in Divine Whispers express the hope, faith, love, fears, burdens, dreams, aspirations and joys of daily living; and the journey of finding and living on purpose. Each poem has a prayer attached to it to help the reader anchor the essence of the communication; and to invite God's divine intervention. It is my prayer and desire that the writings will minister to you wherever you are in your life journey. I pray they will highlight your humanity and reinforce the power of the divine that has been at work from the very beginning of time. Life is fragile and it has the thread of life holding it together. You need to recognise that you have no control over the thread, but you can put your unwavering faith, trust and hope in the one who holds the thread together. God is in control, and He wants you to know you have to let go of your control so that the author and perfecter of your faith; the author of life can do what only He can do in your life.

Life is not served on a bed of roses without thorns, it comes with beauty and pain. There are also times and seasons, as well as time and chance, which are available to everyone. Life requires that you walk circumspectly, so you are in alignment with what God is doing in your life in the different seasons. You need the aerial view from the perspective of God to understand; and unless you are in communion with God, it is difficult to hear His still small voice clearly. Relationship and intimacy are vital for you to hear the heartbeat of the father through the grace of our Lord Jesus Christ and the communion of the Holy Spirit.

Whether you are a person of faith - a Christian or not - welcome to experiencing divine orchestrations. The fact that you have this book in your hand is a sign that God led you to it; it is no coincidence. My invitation to you is, for the period of reading the poems, thoughts and prayers, that you let go of any resistance that may come in the form of doubt, judgement, or scepticism. Trust the moment; you have this book in your hand for a reason. I pray, as you read through, the Holy Spirit will breathe the life of God and minister to you in the way you need. I pray you catch the revelation that God has always, and is always, there for you and with you. God yearns to have a relationship with you.

I don't know what your experience of a father is, but I want you to know God is a loving father and you are His child, and He has loved you with an everlasting love that knows no bounds. He wants to walk this journey of life with you, the way it was originally intended. As you read the texts in this book, give yourself time to reflect, because it may take reading the same poem a few times to really capture the meaning for you. Imagine you are the one the poem is talking about; imagine you are the one contemplating and asking the questions; also imagine you are the one being spoken to. Let your heart and mind be open to receive inspiration, direction, guidance, love, and encouragement. Say the prayers in your own way, which express your heart and your situation. God is waiting on you to call out to Him. He will answer you.

Jeremiah 33:3 - Call to Me, and I will answer you, and show you great and mighty things, which you do not know. NKJV.

Volume 1 of Divine Whispers is themed UNLEASH: Letting go of what is behind to reach out for what is ahead. The poems will remind you about the value and worth you embody; and bring a conscious awareness to what you have been through to be where you are now. More importantly, you will be inspired to reach out for more, regardless of your journey so far; as you let go of every restraint.

God loves you and there is more for you more than you can ever think or imagine. Remain blessed and enjoy reading!

Reflective question

When you think about God, what comes to mind for you?

DIVINE WHISPERS

I hear the inaudible sound
I know things I am not sure how I know
I have wisdom that was not from me
I wonder where all these came from
It can only be from the divine.

Inaudible, yet clear
Unexplainable, yet understandable
Intangible, yet tangible
Invisible, yet visible
It can only be from the divine.

I feel the wave of words coming
I am compelled to pen what comes through
I am a channel available to flow through
I will honour everything that comes too
I am a scribe of the divine.

Whispers become loud when you listen to hear
Whispers touches the heart when you are open to know
Whispers reaches the depths where you allow it to go
Whispers will guide you if you take wisdom from it
Divine whispers will accomplish whatever you let it.

UNDERSTAND
THERE IS MORE
FOR YOU

Understand there is more for you
Know there are depths still unexplored
There are gifts still wrapped in you
Untapped treasure lay in wait for you
You are more than you currently see

1

QUEEN INSIDE OF YOU

Dear Precious Woman.
There is a Queen inside of YOU!
All that you are is in YOU
Your authority lies in Your Own
Uniqueness (YOU).

**TREASURE
INSIDE**

The Queen is the real you, who carries
the essence of your beauty and power
She is the real you, crying out to be fully
expressed
She is the one crying out to you, while you look for her
outside of yourself
She is the one who carries your purpose and potential,
waiting to be unleashed!

Who told you that you are worth nothing?
Yes, YOU are worth everything
Who told you that you have blown it all?
Yes, YOU can rise again
Who told you that it is too late?
Yes, YOU can start now
Get in touch with YOU,
and let the possibilities unfold.

When fear and doubt come,
remember you are a Queen
When you fail and feel vulnerable,
remember to look for the beauty and the lessons
When you feel you are losing it,
remember to never give up
When all else fails, remember,
your circumstance is not your destiny.

Know you have been fearfully and wonderfully made
There is a giant treasure deep inside of YOU
Your key to greatness is found in the essence of who you are
You are innately beautiful and incredibly powerful.

The power to be, lies within you
There can only be one of you
Embrace who God has created you to be, and;
Unlock the treasures of the empire called YOU.

TREASURE WITHIN

Prayer (Queen Inside of YOU)

Loving father, I thank you for reminding me how precious I am. Thank you for highlighting my royalty and reminding me I am a chosen generation. Holy Spirit help me focus inward to see what is already inside of me, instead of looking for outward validation. Help me to be satisfied and content with who I am and my own uniqueness.

I recognise that I can find strength and courage in knowing that you are with me and you empower me to overcome whatever comes against me. Thank you for reminding me that even though I fall many times, I can rise again, according to Proverbs 24:16. Let me never lose sight of how much you love me, in Jesus' name, Amen.

REFLECTION NOTE TO SELF

How different would your life be if you knew and believed in how valuable you are?

2

BEAUTIFUL

You are my precious child
I love you beyond measure
Life may paint a different picture
Doubt may come into the picture
I want you to know, you are beautiful and precious.

Your life is valuable in all ways
I made you complete with treasures
People may say you mean nothing
And think you may amount to nothing
I want you to know, you are beautiful and valuable.

You are delicate yet powerful
I endowed you with strength unspeakable
Falling does not mean defeated
Though the enemy wants you defeated
I want you to know you are beautiful and powerful.

You have access to Heaven's resources
I put in you, solution, and answers
Maybe all you see around is the problem
Not doing anything about it is the problem
I want you to know, you are beautiful and resourceful.

No Devil in Hell can stop you
I made redemption for your dominion
You may believe you are helpless
Truly it is the enemy who is helpless
I want you to know, you are beautiful and unstoppable.

BEAUTIFUL

Prayer (Beautiful)

Gracious Father, I worship you. Everything you made is perfect and you call me beautiful. Thank you for endowing me with beauty, honour, strength and treasure. Thank you for saving and redeeming me through the sacrifice of your dear Son. By your Spirit, O God, give me solutions and answers to the problems I encounter; and give me the courage to keep moving forward, in Jesus' name, Amen.

REFLECTION NOTE TO SELF

How confident would you be if you knew you have the capacity to overcome any challenge you encounter?

3

O CHILD

My love beckons for you
O child, can you see?
When you draw closer to me
My presence is forever near
I am closer than you think.

My heart beats for you
O child, can you feel?
When you abide in me for sure
My life will freely flow in you
I am available more than you think.

My will yearns for you
O child, can you perceive?
When your will aligns with mine
There is no limitation for you
I have more for you than you know.

My forgiveness is available for you
O child, can you receive?
When you lay it all down with me
The enemy has no hold on you
You have been set free, you need to know.

My throne waits for you
O child, can you come?
When you lay your life on the altar
The holy of holies is a place for you
You can come boldly without fear.

O CHILD

Prayer (O Child)

Eternal rock of ages I worship you. Thank you for your love, your grace and for your mercies that endure forever. You are full of compassion, and you desire to have a relationship with me. Thank you, Lord, for the expression of your love to me in many ways. Help me to see, feel, perceive, receive, and come to you. Help me to remember you are always beckoning to me and help me to reach out and receive your love; in Jesus' name, Amen.

REFLECTION NOTE TO SELF

How open are you to receiving and giving love?

4

ACCEPTED

I could never earn your love
Freely I have been given
My imperfection not withstanding
I am accepted just the way I am.

Your mercy I could never understand
You make it new every morning
Regardless of my shortcomings
I am accepted just the way I am.

How patient can you be?
You beckon gently for my attention
No matter how long it takes
I am accepted just the way I am.

Taught by an all-knowing God
Your ways are higher than mine
Even when I do not understand
I am accepted just the way I am.

You fight all my battles
The Lord of Hosts is your name
I sometimes don't see what you are doing
I am accepted just the way I am.

Your saving grace astounds me
You gave your life all for me
Though I was dead in my sin
Your amazing grace rescued me
I am accepted just the way I am.

ACCEPTED

Prayer (Accepted)

Thank you, Lord, for accepting me just the way I am. Everything about me is all because of you. Your grace, your love, your patience, your mercy, and your understanding have brought me this far. I am eternally grateful to you. Empower me by your Spirit to always come boldly to you; when things are great and when things are not great. It makes no difference to you because you see me as righteous because of Jesus Christ; and I am accepted just the way I am. Amen.

REFLECTION NOTE TO SELF

Have you fully accepted and embraced all of who you are?

5

BLESSED

You have called me blessed
Therefore, I am a blessing
Everything about me is fruitful
Everything good around me shall multiply
Your declaration about me is amplified.

You have called me blessed
Therefore, I am a blessing
Nothing about me can be cursed
Nothing good around me shall remain small
Your favour upon me is intensified.

You have called me blessed
Therefore, I am a blessing
Those things behind me I forget
Those things before me I pursue
Your mercy towards me is magnified.

You have called me blessed
Therefore, I am a blessing
Everything you made me I embrace
Everything you gave me I shall steward
Your generosity towards me is multiplied.

You have called me blessed
Therefore, I am a blessing
Everywhere you take me you ordained
Everywhere you lead me is the way
Your counsel towards me is simplified.

BLESSED

Prayer (Blessed)

Mighty God, I worship you. I lift you high and give glory, honour and adoration to you. All blessings come from You and no one can curse who you have blessed. I thank you Lord for calling me blessed. Thank you for your favour, mercy, grace and your unfailing love. Give me a heart of gratitude and the wisdom to always count my blessings, in Jesus' name, Amen.

REFLECTION NOTE TO SELF

How differently would you approach life if you know you are blessed?

6

WORTHY

See yourself as worthy, because you are
See yourself as deserving, because you are
You may not yet believe it, but still, you are
Only believe in who says you are.

Know yourself as worthy, because you are
Know yourself as deserving, because you are
You may not yet understand it, but still, you are
Only seek understanding from who says you are.

Accept yourself as worthy, because you are
Accept yourself as deserving, because you are
You may not yet feel like it, but still, you are
Only receive acceptance from who says you are.

Live your life as worthy, because you are
Live your life as deserving, because you are
You may be unfamiliar with this, but still, you are
Only draw strength from the one who says you are.

You are worthy, you are worthy
Again, I say you are.
You are deserving, you are deserving
Again, I say you are.

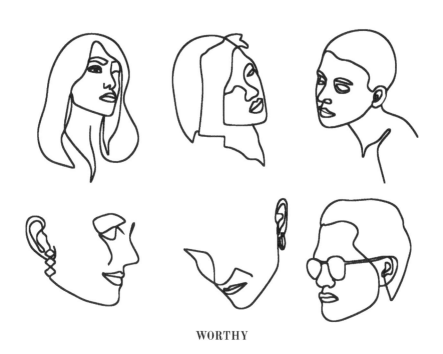

WORTHY

Prayer (Worthy)

Dear God, I thank you for your words of assurance and encouragement. Thank you for calling me worthy and deserving of every good thing you have for me. When I feel unworthy and undeserving because of my experiences and circumstance, help me remember you gave your all for me, in Jesus' name, Amen.

REFLECTION NOTE TO SELF

How different would you be as a person if you stopped listening to, and believing the voices telling you that you are not worthy; and choose to believe you are worthy?

7

YOU CALL ME BY NAME

Did I hear you call me by name?
Why would a mighty God take notice of me?
Who am I to deserve your attention?
It's your divine love that qualified me.

Did you know me before I was formed?
What purpose could I ever fulfil?
Who am I to be worth being born?
It's your divine purpose that qualified me.

Did you make a way to save me?
Why does relationship matter to you?
Who am I to deserve redemption?
It's your divine will that qualified me.

Did you anoint me for good works?
Why would you give me so many gifts?
Who am I to be used by you?
It's your divine grace that qualified me.

Did you arise to fight my battle?
Why would the Lord of Host stand for me?
Who am I to be assured of victory?
It's your divine power that qualified me.

YOU CALL ME BY NAME

Prayer (You Call Me by Name)

Father God I stand in awe of you. Thank you for creating me and loving me so much. Nothing is too big or too small to do for me. When I stop to think about everything you have done for me, I cannot help but wonder what man means to you, and more specifically, what I mean to you. Thank you for calling me by name, thank you for knowing me, thank you for saving me, thank you for anointing me and thank you for fighting my battles. What more can I ask from a God who knows me and sees me. Help me, by your spirit, to be confident in who I am in you, in Jesus' name, Amen.

REFLECTION NOTE TO SELF

Have you ever wondered about God's love for you?

NEVER ALLOW THE PAST OR PRESENT RESTRAIN YOU

Never allow the past or present restrain you
The force they exert can overwhelm you
Appreciate the blessings of every season
Remember the change that is set to come
You are not meant to remain stuck

U**N**LEASH

8

GOODBYE YESTERDAY

When I look back in time
I see a trail of my past
History lurks in the shadow
Scared to shine a light
I quickly want to say
Goodbye yesterday.

When fixated on yesterday
It is hard to see where I am
New opportunities all around
Reluctant to take a chance
Constantly telling myself
I messed it up yesterday.

When I hold on to guilt of the past
I remain stuck in time
A whole new life beckons
Waiting to create a new story
Self-forgiveness is vital
To leave the past in yesterday.

When I turn my gaze on you
I find a new lease on life
My ashes turn into beauty
Gems of wisdom are revealed
Portions I want to erase
Are battle scars of yesterday.

When all is said and done,
I can confidently say
Goodbye yesterday
Today is a new day
I welcome my tomorrow
My days are in your hands
Rest assured, I am.

**GOODBYE
YESTERDAY**

Prayer (Goodbye Yesterday)

O Lord my God, You are the same yesterday, today and forever. Thank you for your promise of a better today and tomorrow than my yesterday. Thank you for your word that confirms that the days ahead of me are greater and better than the former. I can look forward with excitement knowing no matter how bad or great yesterday was, today can be better and tomorrow can be spectacular. Empower me, by your Spirit, to forget those things which are behind and reach forward to those things which are ahead, in Jesus' name, Amen.

REFLECTION NOTE TO SELF

What do you need to let go from your past, so that you can become unstuck and move forward?

9

SCAR

Your scar is the badge that qualifies you
No need to hide it, because it is real
Your scar authorizes you to speak into situations
Show me your pain and will believe your gain.

Your scar is a proof of your healing
All humans are broken, and that is for real
Your scar indicates you were once wounded
I know you are restored, when you can show me.

Your scar is a reminder of your victory
You have been qualified by life, that is real
Your scar tells me you have a battle plan
I will let you stand with me, you have been here before.

Your scar acknowledges your imperfection
You can't make it on your own, that is so real
Your scar necessitates the balm everyday
The anointing will flow, when you are secure firmly in him.

No longer ashamed of my scars
No longer afraid of imperfections of life
No longer hold on to the pain of my scars
No longer will I withhold the blessings from my scars.

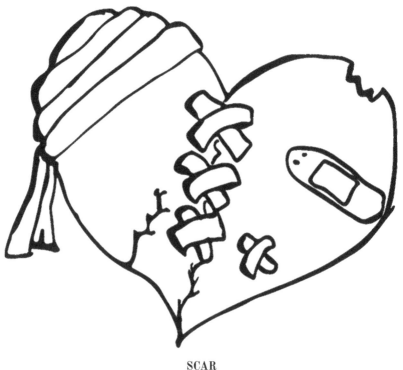

SCAR

Prayer (Scar)

You are a perfect God who loves imperfect people. Thank you for your everlasting love that reaches to the highest height and to the deepest depth. Thank you for making provision for healing and restoration. Thank you for all the lessons learnt through the scars we pick up through life. The next time I look at my scar, remind me it is the badge that qualifies me. Amen.

REFLECTION NOTE TO SELF

What has your scar qualified and authorised you to do?

10

KEEP MOVING

I feel stuck and closed in
I see no way out
I cry out and look up
You said, keep moving!

I feel fear and paralysed
I don't know what to do
I complain and lament
You said, keep moving!

I can't go back or forward
I am in a hard place
I lose hope and settle down
You said, keep moving!

I look right and look left
I see no one to help
I sit still with self-pity
You said, keep moving!

I searched high and searched low
I have no answer in sight
I quit seeking and knocking
You said, keep moving!

When I see no way out
When I don't know what to do
When I am in a hard place
When I see no one to help
When I have no answer in sight
Help me to keep moving!

KEEP MOVING

Prayer (Keep Moving!)

Great and Mighty God, I worship and adore you. You are my very present help in time of need. When I am busy moving through life in my own strength, help me to remember I need empowerment by your spirit to keep moving. My strength will fail me, but I can do all things through Christ who strengthens me. Amen.

REFLECTION NOTE TO SELF

In what area of your life do you need to keep moving in spite of the current circumstances?

11

IN THE END

When I see my mistakes
You see who you made
You yearn to hear me call out
The book of my life is in order
Who you say I am, is what matters in the end.

When I see no way out
You see Jesus is the way
You yearn for me to step in
The path made straight before me
Where your Spirit leads me, is what matters in the end.

When I see my fears
You see the courage in me
You yearn for me to conquer
No one can stand against me
Those who are with me, is what matters in the end.

When I see my weakness
You see your strength made perfect
You yearn for me to draw near
The fountain of life refreshes
What you can do through me, is what matters in the end.

When I see my lack
You see your riches in glory
You yearn for me to ask you
Jehovah Jireh is your name
Trusting you for everything, is what matters in the end.

When I see nothing in me
You see me and know me
You yearn for me to find you
All of my heart will seek you
Knowing you intimately, is what matters in the end.

IN THE END

Prayer (In the end)

Lord, I thank you for who you are and all you have done for me. Life can be tough sometimes but what matters in the end is what you say about me, what you see in me, what you have for me and what you can do in and through me. You have the final say and that is what matters. Lord help me not to believe the lies of the enemy, and give me the courage to silence the enemy, in Jesus' name, Amen.

REFLECTION NOTE TO SELF

When all is said and done, what matters for you in the end?

12

COURAGEOUS HEART

The issues of life flow out of the heart
To know who I am, is to master my heart
With the heart we believe
With the heart we also doubt
A courageous heart is one that takes a stand.

The core of my being is placed within my heart
To experience who I am, is to lay down my heart
With the heart we receive
With the heart we also give
A courageous heart is one that dares to live.

The beauty of love is expressed from the heart
To embrace who I am, is to trust my heart
With the heart we give love
With the heart we also hate
A courageous heart is one that choose to love.

The seat of knowing is right within my heart
To express who I am, is to follow my heart
With the heart we will seek
With the heart we also find
A courageous heart is one that is not afraid to ask.

COURAGEOUS HEART

Prayer (Courageous heart)

Lord, I thank you for creating me in your own image and after your own likeness. Thank you for putting a heart in your creation. Thank you for the portal that the heart is, and how it helps me connect with you. Thank you, Lord, because I can know, I can love, I can believe, I can receive and I can conceive with and in my heart. Help me Holy Spirit to yield my heart to you and help me to be courageous at all times, in Jesus' name, Amen.

REFLECTION NOTE TO SELF

What would courage have you do today and in the future?

13

THE STORY I TELL MYSELF

What I believe is what I permit
The unveiling of the world within
How come I am the way I am
Could it be the story I tell myself?

When I choose to learn, I choose to grow
The enlarging of the depths within
I go a mile for what I desire
I am the story I tell myself.

Having the confidence to believe
The drawing out of the wisdom within
Courage or fear, what is it gonna be?
I choose the story I tell myself.

I tell myself things all the time
Then wonder why I do things all the time
I create my experience, a thought at a time
Powerful is the story I tell myself.

When all has been said and done
I am who God created me to be
I will live, love and die being me
This is the story I tell myself.

THE STORY I TELL MYSELF

Prayer (The Story I tell Myself)

Precious Father, I thank you for reminding me about the power of my thoughts and what I say to myself. Help me pay attention to my thoughts and empower me to hold every negative thought captive. Help me to get your words into my spirit and soul so that I can focus on words that are true, lovely and of good report. Empower me to think good thoughts and speak words of life to myself. Grant me wisdom and courage to be who you have created me to be, in Jesus' name, Amen.

REFLECTION NOTE TO SELF

What disempowering story have you been telling yourself?

14

A DATE WITH MY FUTURE

You knew me before you formed me
Everything about me existed before me
The number of my days preceded my coming
Every step I take is mapped out before me
What will a date with my future tell me?

Every day of my life unfolds before me
The person I am is who you called me
Challenges of life can be deforming
I meet a different me every stage you take me
What will a date with my future show me?

I want to know the details of everything you tell me
Walking in faith is the currency you showed me
I learned to act on the last instruction you gave me
The more I trust you, the less I need to know
What will a date with my future teach me?

I focus my mind on counsel from above
Everything that is made is not without you
Getting back to the beginning when you made me
I am transformed from glory to glory
How will a date with my future change me?

Eye has not seen what you see inside me
Ear has not heard what is possible for me
My heart has not captured all the plans you have for me
Your love and purposes establish my calling
Where will a date with my future lead me?

A DATE WITH MY FUTURE

Prayer (A Date with my Future)

Age to age you stand O God, and time is in your hands. Thank you, that You knew me before You formed me in my mother's womb. Thank you for ordaining every single day of my life. As You take me through life and time, help me to see your plan and purpose unfold according to your pre-determinate counsel. Help me, by your Spirit to believe that the days ahead of me are greater and better than the former days. Take me from glory to glory, strength to strength, and from wisdom to wisdom. I decree and declare by the power in the name and blood of Jesus, that my future is brighter than my past and present, in Jesus' name, Amen.

REFLECTION NOTE TO SELF

What steps would you be taking now, if you knew everything would work out in your future?

LET GOD BE YOUR STRENGTH

Let God be your strength
You are not meant to do life alone
When God helps you
Nothing can stop you
Stand in that confidence, you can't go wrong

15

STILL ABIDE

You set my feet on solid ground
My life you hold in the palm of your hands
How then shall I not mercy find?
When love and kindness still abide.

You set my mind on things on high
My hopes and dreams in you are found
How then shall I not uplifting find?
When grace and favour still abide.

You set my heart on what's on yours
My pains and fears exchanged for joy
How then shall I not comfort find?
When peace and forgiveness still abide.

You set my face on your mercy throne
My guilt and shame you set aside
How then shall I not glory find?
When righteousness and justice still abide.

Your love, kindness and mercy finds me
There is grace and favour for my lifting
Your peace and forgiveness comforts me
In righteousness and justice, your glory remain.

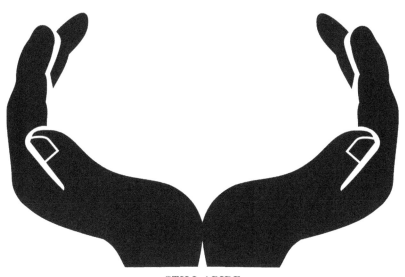

STILL ABIDE

Prayer (Still Abide)

Father God, you are faithful and remain the same. You are full of grace, love, kindness, and mercy. I thank you for your favor, your forgiveness, peace, righteousness, and justice. Thank you, Lord, that I can always count on and rely on you. Holy spirit, help me to remain when I feel like quitting; remind me that you remain the same and still abide, in Jesus' name, Amen.

REFLECTION NOTE TO SELF

Did you know you can rely on God's character and integrity to uphold you?

16

I KNOW

I know who it is that made me
The same is the one that called me
I can't go wrong if I trust you
I know I am yours forever.

I know you live inside me
Your voice directs and guides me
I won't be lost if I let you
I know I'll end up where you want me.

I know you watch over me
Your eyes keep me from falling
I won't be safe without you
I know to stay where you keep me.

I know how much you love me
Everything about you tells me
I won't be here without you
I know how far you brought me.

I know you fight my battles.
You give me strength to push through
I win when you go before me
I know to trust what you tell me.

I know you call me blessed
I know that all is well
I know you are there for me
I know I am yours.

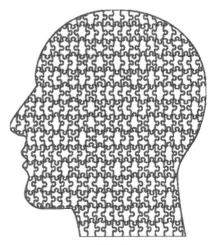

I KNOW

Prayer (I Know)

All knowing God, I know you are faithful and mighty. Your love is beyond comprehension and your care I could never understand. Thank you for your kindness and mercy towards me. Thank you for leading and guiding me. When my heart is overwhelmed, let what I know about you keep me going, in Jesus' name, Amen.

REFLECTION NOTE TO SELF

What are the things you know for sure?

17

WHY

Why do I feel this way?
Tight in the chest, heart beating fast
Thoughts racing through my mind
At the speed of light, can't catch a breath
No wonder I feel this way.

Why do I see this way?
Eyes opened wide, moving to and fro
Looking everywhere to catch a glimpse
With preconceived ideas, can't envision a thing
No wonder I see this way.

Why do I speak this way?
Tongue in mouth ready to fire
Words are bubbling inside my head
When understanding is lacking; don't know what to say
No wonder I speak this way.

Why do I love this way?
Fire in my bones, emotion running high
There is so much I want to give
When I focus on myself, don't know how to choose
No wonder I love this way.

My feelings are there to serve me
Let me see through the eyes of my spirit
When I speak, let life be what comes through
In your love, I can do all things.

WHY

Prayer (Why)

Dear Lord, I adore you. You are an unquestionable God, yet I can come to you when I have questions. When I have a million whys, help me to turn to you for the voice of reason. I silence the voice of fear, the voice of doubt and the voice of despair by the power in the blood of Jesus. Help me to guard my heart and my mind in Christ, in Jesus' name, Amen.

REFLECTION NOTE TO SELF

Who do you turn to when you have questions?

18

FOREVER SURE

When the wind of life blows me around
You are my firm anchor
Though my heart be shaken
Your love forever affirms me.

When I am confused and don't know what to do
You are my confident assurance
Though I have a million questions
Your word is forever settled.

When I feel lost and alone
You are my sweet comforter
Though my soul be weary
Your outstretched arms forever embrace me.

When I get to the end of myself
You start your mighty work in me
Though my mind may not comprehend
Your power forever creates the change.

When I worry about the future
You know the end from the beginning
Though I may not yet see what you see
Your promises are forever sure.

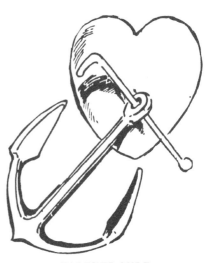

FOREVER SURE

Prayer (Forever Sure)

Dear God, I am grateful that you are consistent, and you never fail. You are always there and always near. Everything about you is forever sure. Grant me the courage to trust in the integrity of your character, which has remained the same from age to age. Help me to know, that even when I don't understand what you are doing, I can be assured that all is well; in Jesus' name, Amen.

REFLECTION NOTE TO SELF

What is your anchor when things in your life becomes shaken?

19

WAIT

When you tell me to wait
I sometimes don't feel the need
Nevertheless, when I wait
My heart is strengthened.

When you tell me to wait
I sometimes don't comprehend
Nevertheless, when I wait
Word comes from you to inform me.

When you tell me to wait
I sometimes don't know what to expect
Nevertheless, when I wait
Your goodness finds me.

When you tell me to wait
I sometimes don't understand
Nevertheless, when I wait
I receive wisdom at your feet.

When you tell me to wait
I sometimes don't see what you see
Nevertheless, when I wait
I receive vision at the appointed time.

When you tell me to wait
I sometimes don't know why
Nevertheless, when I wait
I obtain your beautiful promise.

In the place of waiting;
Virtues flow and, deep calls to deep
Strength is renewed and, strongholds are broken
Foundations are shaken and, life is restored
Destiny is found and, blueprints revealed
When my heart yearns for an answer now
May I always remember to wait.

WAIT

Prayer (Wait)

All knowing God, I reverence you. I acknowledge that waiting for a word from you is better than rushing to get things done. I pray that in the place of waiting, my strength is renewed, my eyes are opened, and my wisdom is increased. Help me by your spirit, to be patient and sustain the staying power. Help me to see and understand that waiting is a part of the process and give me the wisdom to know that fighting the process is counterproductive. Align my perspective to yours, so that I can see things just the way you see them, in Jesus' name, Amen.

REFLECTION NOTE TO SELF

What would it take for you to wait, when it is the last thing you want to do?

20

JOY

When I think about your love
I see a heart that cares about me
My shortcomings not withstanding
When I remain in your beautiful presence,
Joy everlasting will be my portion.

When I hear your voice call out to me
I know the sound that shows me the way
My knowledge not withstanding
When I trust the counsel of the one who leads me,
Joy unspeakable will make me wonder.

When I taste and see your goodness
I am convinced of your favour towards me
My undeserving not withstanding
When I humbly receive your blessings,
Joy immeasurable will be my experience.

When I walk by the faith you gave me
I know a new world will open before me
My understanding not withstanding
When I hold on to your promises,
Joy remarkable will be my testimony,

In your presence, is fullness of joy
In your counsel, is wisdom evermore
In your blessings, no sorrow is found
Your promises are yes and Amen.

JOY

Prayer (Joy)

There is fullness of joy in your presence, Mighty God. Let the joy that you give be my strength. Regardless of the circumstances I face, let my heart and mind be secure in you; and let your peace rest upon me. Your ways are perfect, Mighty God. Your goodness and mercy shall follow me all the days of my life. Lead me, teach me and guide me into your perfect will. Amen.

REFLECTION NOTE TO SELF

What does joy look like for you?

21

UNSTOPPABLE

Nothing is gonna stop me
I refuse to be overtaken
My faith remains unshaken
I am unstoppable.

Your promises are sure to benefit me
One by one, they rescue me
I stand on the rock of ages
I am unstoppable.

There are grounds for me to conquer
Day by day, I advance unhindered
Barriers in my way surrender
I am unstoppable.

Mountains disappear at my order
Angels appear at my call
I am forever an overcomer
I am unstoppable.

When I fall, I will rise again
When I fail, I will try again
When I weep, I will Laugh again
I refuse to be hindered
I am unstoppable.

UNSTOPPABLE

Prayer (Unstoppable)

Dear God, I thank you for your power that is at work in me. Thank you that I can move on in life with the knowledge that you are with me. According to Romans 8:3, If you are for me, no one can be against me. Help me remember that facing opposition does not mean I have to be defeated. Help me to always look to you for my strength and confidence. Let me never lose my faith and trust in you. Help me to always remember that I am an overcomer, through Jesus Christ, Amen.

REFLECTION NOTE TO SELF

What have you allowed to stop you?

ELIMINATE FEAR FROM YOUR LIFE

Eliminate fear from your life
You have power, love, and sound mind
No more playing small
You have every reason to step up
Destinies are waiting for you

22

PERFECT LOVE

Who am I without love?
If I know not love, I know not I, for I am love
I am made by love, made with love, and made for love
Without love, I am a mere shadow of myself.

A life without love is like the dryness of a desert
A love awakening, ushers in the freshness
A life with love is like a refreshing oasis
It is the place that represents home.

Love is the gateway of the heart, through which all virtues flow
To deny love is to deny self, and to deny self, is to restrict self
Throw open the flood gates, and let love freely flow
For where there is love, there is freedom.

Freedom to give and receive love
Freedom of full expression without fear
Freedom to choose love and reject hate
Freedom to live a life you love.

Love bears and Love heals
Love gives and Love receives
Love is patient and Love is kind
Perfect love casts out all fear.

PERFECT LOVE

Prayer (Perfect Love)

Father of love and light, I worship you. I thank you, because you are the very essence of love and you created me out of love. Lord, I ask that you open my heart and my mind to understand and comprehend the extent of your love for me. Help me to receive and embody your love. Let your love shine in and through me in all my interactions and encounters, in Jesus' name, Amen.

REFLECTION NOTE TO SELF

How does love show up for you?

23

WEEP NOT

Crying to sleep, when all hope seems lost
Away from all eyes, yet he sees my tears
Darkness lingers through the long cold night
In the sight of daybreak, hope comes alive
Weep not my child, joy comes in the morning.

Stuck in one place, I don't know where to turn
Lost in confusion, but he knows exactly where I'm at
A fork in the road, I need wisdom to know
When my eyes are fixed on him, I can see the way
Weep not my child, I make a way in the wilderness.

Tormented by regrets, how could this be?
Though I lost my way, his purpose remains
Messed up, beat up, didn't think I had a chance
My life in his hands, he makes all things new
Weep not my child, your future is not like your past.

The war in my mind, seeks to take me out
My thoughts may run wild, his truth is ever sure
In the midst of raging war, seen and unseen
Those on my side are more than I can see
Weep not my child, victory is already yours

The worries of life are drowning like the sea
Though the tides are high, his love anchors my soul
Overwhelmed by fear, riding against the tides
When he calls out my name, I can walk upon the sea
Weep not my child, I am taking you to the other side.

WEEP NOT

Prayer (Weep Not)

Compassionate and caring God, I appreciate you. I thank you for always being there to wipe away my tears. When circumstances of life push me to tears, help me to remember not to weep in defeat. Let my weeping be a sign of brokenness because you cannot despise a broken and a contrite spirit. Open my eyes to see the victory that is already mine and to know that all will be well in the end, in Jesus' name, Amen.

REFLECTION NOTE TO SELF

Who do you allow to wipe your tears?

24

I SEE

I see mountains melt, at the sound of your voice
I am confident no problem can overwhelm me
Though life throws many weights on me
I am more than a conqueror in all of these.

I see dead bones come alive, at the touch of your breath
I know your life will always give me strength
No matter what lies ahead to accomplish
The power that raised Christ from the dead lives in me.

I see curses and chains broken, by the power of your name
No stronghold or power can keep me bound
When the accuser wants judgement against me
I am set free because of You.

I see poverty and lack wiped away, by your blood
My needs are met by your riches in glory
Regardless of what I currently see
I am called blessed because of You.

I see all tongues and tribes call out to You
You hold the world in the palm of your hands
Despite the agenda and plan of Hell
Your kingdom come, your will be done.

Mountains melt
Dead bones come alive
Curses and chains are broken
Poverty and lack wiped away
All tongues and tribes call out to You
Give me the heart to believe, so I can hold what I see.

I SEE

Prayer (I See)

Mighty God, you hold the whole world in your hand. You are full of glory, power and might. You are the giver of life. Give me eyes that see beyond the obvious and help me see things just the way you see them. When the fight for my soul rages, let me not be moved by circumstance around me; help me to only be moved by what you say about things. Empower me by your Holy Spirit to discern and to access your wisdom in all situations. Help me to remember that your power is made perfect in my weakness. The same power that raised Christ from the dead lives in me, Amen.

REFLECTION NOTE TO SELF

Is what you currently see, what you want to eventually hold?

25

I WONDER

The mind holds the images for our lives
The mouth speaks the images to life
Oh, what a creative power we have
I wonder how much aware we are.

When the mind thinks a thought of fear
The mouth will say, I am doomed for life
Little do you know this is a trap
I wonder how much aware we are.

When you renew your mind with light
Your perspective will change in time
The mouth will begin to speak life
I wonder how much aware we are.

Enlighten my mind to behold my thoughts
Align my emotions and will to thine
Then my soul will prosper and be whole
I wonder how much aware we are

You search the heart to know the mind
The tower of the mind transmits the life
We must guard our hearts with all we have
I wonder how much aware we are.

I WONDER

Prayer (I wonder)

Dear God, I thank you for my life and how far you have brought me. Thank you, Lord, for giving me a mind and a mouth, and for the power they both have to create my experiences. Help me to use my mind and my mouth to honour you in my life. Holy Spirit, I ask that you help me to be more aware of my thoughts and more in control of my speech, in Jesus' name, Amen.

REFLECTION NOTE TO SELF

What experiences are you creating with your mind and mouth?

26

REST

Why lose sleep, when your keeper never sleeps
Day or night, you don't have to fear
He watches over you with utmost care
The true proof of trust is a soul fully at rest.

Why lose peace, when you know the Prince of Peace
Turmoil or calm, you don't have to freak
He carries your burden through the times
The true proof of trust is a soul fully at rest.

Why lose hope, when you know the Giver of Hope
Up or down, you don't have to lose your grip
He anchors your life on a firm and solid rock
The true proof of trust is a soul fully at rest.

Why lose joy, when his presence has fullness of joy
Sorrow and suffering, you don't have to worry
He satisfies your heart with pleasures evermore
The true proof of trust is a soul fully at rest.

Why lose faith, when you know a faithful God
Seen or unseen, you don't have to doubt
He holds nothing back when your confidence is sure in him
The true proof of trust is a soul fully at rest.

REST

Prayer (Rest)

Heavenly Father, you are a faithful God. You are true and you remain the same. I thank you because you never sleep nor slumber. I thank you, that I can have fullness of joy in your presence. Thank you, that you are the Prince of Peace and the Giver of Hope. Let me enter your rest and let your peace surround me, in Jesus' name, Amen.

REFLECTION NOTE TO SELF

What helps you to rest in the midst of unrest?

27

I RUN TO YOU

I walk through the journey of life
Step by step, I conquer the grounds
When my world is in turmoil
I run to you, my safe refuge.

I live my life daily for you
One by one, I deal with all the cares
When my mind is overwhelmed
I run to you, my perfect peace.

I do the things you ask of me
Bit by bit, I do my part
When I feel lost and lack direction
I run to you, my secure guide.

I fully commit to your will
Leap by leap, I stretch myself
When my soul and body is weary
I run to you, my merciful healer.

I take responsibility for what you gave to me
Day to day, meeting the needs
When my supply is running out
I run to you, my great provider.

I take steps of faith every day
Night by night, I evaluate the day
When my heart is fearful
I run to you, my sweet comfort.

I live with the knowledge of who you are
Through and through, I follow you
When the world asks who I serve
I run to you, my loving God.

RUN TO YOU

Prayer (I Run to You)

Loving God, I am grateful that you never change, and you remain the same. Thank you for the assurance of knowing you will always be there for me when I run to you. Thank you for being a safe refuge and a place of peace and comfort. I am grateful that you provide for my needs, you heal me, and you guide me. Help me by your Holy Spirit to remain in you and to follow you all the days of my life in Jesus' name, Amen.

REFLECTION NOTE TO SELF

Where do you run to for comfort and assurance?

28

YOU ARE

You are great and you remain the same
Nothing will ever compare to your love
I searched high, I searched low
I looked wide all around me
All I see is your amazing grace.

You are my God and my redeemer
I would have been lost without you
You called me, you chose me
I am in awe of your eternal plan
All I know is your amazing love.

You are my glory and you lift my head
I would have been defeated without you
You gifted me, you purposed me
I am who I am because of you
All I find is your amazing peace.

You are strong and mighty in battle
You trained my hands to war and fingers to fight
You prepare me and You go ahead of me
All I have to do is follow your lead
Every battle with You is a done deal.

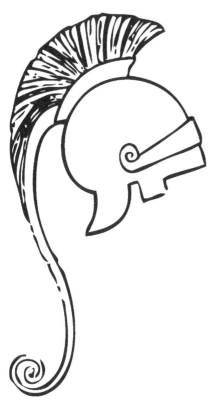

YOU ARE

Prayer (You Are)

Thank you, Lord for your amazing grace, love and peace. You are God and you never change. Thank you for your plan and purpose for my life, thank you for being my guide and my shield. Thank you for teaching me to fight a good fight to obtain the victory you already won. Help me to seek you with all my heart so that I can find you at all times. In Jesu's name, Amen.

REFLECTION NOTE TO SELF

What does God mean to you?

ALIGN YOUR WILL TO GOD'S WILL

Align your will to God's will
Submit yourself and draw close to Him
In the fullness of time, His plan will unfold
What is in stock for you will amaze you
Don't give up, keep your hope alive

29

IN YOU ALONE

How could I not know how much You love me?
When everything about you tells of your love
You love me so much and gave me life
In You alone, I find my place.

How could I not know how powerful my God is?
When he is the Lord of the Heavenly Host
Those with me are more than those against me
In You alone, I make my boast.

How could I not know You can do exploits?
When nothing is impossible with You in charge
I can do all things because of your spirit within me
In You alone, I find my strength.

How could I not know You deserve all my heart?
Any other way has proven futile
Relying on You has never failed me
In You alone I put my trust.

How could I not know You are my only source?
Staying connected to the true vine is a must
I can't live life without the author of my life
In You alone, I have my being.

In You alone, I find my place
In You alone, I make my boast
In You alone, I find my strength
In You alone, I put my trust
In You alone, I have my being.

IN YOU ALONE

Prayer (In You Alone)

Author of Life, I exalt your Holy Name. No one else can compare to You. Your everlasting love knows no bounds, your amazing grace is beyond compare. I thank you, that I can find and have all I need in You alone. Help me to always remember that I am nothing without You and cannot be anything except by You. You are great and mighty, powerful, and strong. Thank you that You are all for me and you fight for me, in Jesus' name, Amen.

REFLECTION NOTE TO SELF

What is the one thing you have an unshaken confidence in?

30

WHO AM I WITHOUT YOU

Who am I without you?
A shadow to say the least
When my anchor has no hold
Stability I cannot hold.

Who am I without you?
A freelancer in the journey of life
When your guidance is far from me
Living on purpose will be a dream.

Who am I without you?
A river without its source
When connection with you is lost
My soul will die, though silently.

Who am I without you?
A traveller without a map
When your direction is hidden from me
Where I end up will be my will.

Help me find stability in you
Help me live my life on purpose
Help my soul come alive in you
Help me remain at the centre of your will.

WHO AM I WITHOUT YOU

Prayer (Who am I without You)

King of Glory, I worship and honour you. I acknowledge I am nothing without you. You are the source of my life, my hope and my being. Let me remain grafted in you, so that the life that flows out of me comes from you. Let me not be deceived into believing I don't need you; and let me not miss my way. I pray I am always guided by your will as I daily lay down my will. Let your Kingdom come and your will be done in my life, in Jesus' name, Amen.

REFLECTION NOTE TO SELF

Who is your identity connected to?

31

THE MAKING OF A VESSEL

When fear of the unknown grips me,
I need to remember I am going through a process
The furnace of affliction yields beauty
Repeated refining, is a warranty in the making
Inhale, take a deep breath, and stay on the potter's wheel.

When the impatience of the 'in between' cripples me
May I remember I need to remain on the journey
The valley of life yields complete surrender
Staying the course, is endurance in the making
Look up, focus on God, and let Him lead the way.

When the pain of becoming a vessel hits me
Let me remember that I have been chosen
The training ground equips for the calling
Pressure allowed, is transformation in the making
Stand still, remain grounded, and yield to His moulding.

When the weight of the mantle comes upon me
I need to remember who does the lifting
Communion with Him transfers the virtue
Abiding in the secret place, guarantees connection
Arise, rely on him to do His work through you.

Exhale, nothing is wrong with you
It is the price of the calling
It is the making of a vessel;
Fit for the master's use.

THE MAKING OF A VESSEL

Prayer (The Making of a Vessel)

Thank you, Lord, for knowing me, choosing me and calling me. I thank you for the purpose you have for my life. Thank you for moulding and shaping me into a vessel fit for your use. Thank you for building character in me. When I feel the crushing and the pressing, help me to remember that you are making something of value in the process. Empower me by your Holy Spirit to remain on the potter's wheel, in Jesus' name, Amen.

REFLECTION NOTE TO SELF

Are you submitting to or are you terminating the process of your making?

32

I RUN MY RACE

I run my race and fulfil my calling
Day by day, I do what you tell me
I know you lead me every step you take me
Your ways are higher than mine
I cannot afford to doubt you.

I run my race as best as I can
Although the end will justify the means
I rest assured because of the way you have shown me
You have shaped my path to fit me
I cannot afford to meddle.

I run my race until the end
Finishing is better than starting
I have the grace and strength to go through
I mount up with wings to soar like an eagle
I cannot afford to settle.

I will finish my race if I stay on course
Master every distraction that entices
Knowing I can rise again if I fall
There will be no stopping me on my journey.

I RUN MY RACE

Prayer (I run my race)

My Father and my God, I sing praises to You. You have created me and called me for your purpose at such a time as this. Help me to run my race and stay the course no matter what life throws at me. I thank you for always being there loving and guiding me through this life. Thank you for giving me the courage and the strength to keep going. Thank you, that even when I fall, I can rise again. Empower me by your spirit to run this race till the end, in Jesus' name, Amen.

REFLECTION NOTE TO SELF

What does your race look like and what is keeping you on track?

33

TIME

Time tests

Can the truth in your heart stand the test of time?
Can you go the mile and still stand?
Trust the author of time to help you stand
Give it time, because life happens in time.

Time tells

Who knows what tomorrow will bring?
Keep the momentum of what you believe
Hold on to the hope of a greater future
Give it time, because life happens in time.

Time reveals

That not seen, will be revealed in time
Faith at work will bring it to pass
Unbelief and doubt should be out of your heart
Give it time, because life happens in time.

Time heals

Pain released will heal in time
Balm of God will accomplish the task
Restoration will come as you let go of the past
Give it time, because life happens in time.

Time assures

Every journey begins as a moment in time
Assurance of an end, comes with knowing the times
Alpha omega took care of every step
Give it time, because life happens in time.

Time approves

The calling on your life will be tested by time
Can you steward your gifts and be ready for time
You will receive the reward if you do not give up
Give it time, because life happens in time.

LIFE HAPPENS IN TIME

Prayer (Time)

Dear God, I thank you for giving us the gift of time even though you exist outside of time. Thank you, Lord, for creating times and seasons and making time abound for every purpose under the sun. Grant me the patience to wait for things that require time, grant me the wisdom to value the time I have been gifted; and help me to persevere in the test of time. Help me to be assured that in the due season and at the appointed time, your promises will come to pass; in Jesus' name, Amen.

REFLECTION NOTE TO SELF

How are you stewarding the time you have been gifted?

34

ONLY YOU

My soul yearns for connection
I searched high and I searched low
Until I encountered your love
Now I can confidently say
Only You can satisfy.

I want to be the best I can
All hope seems lost the more I try
Until your power transformed me
Now I can confidently say
Only You can change a life.

I desire increase from my labour
I tried hard, but seem to miss the mark
Until your favour worked for me
Now I can confidently say
Only You can multiply.

I want my life to matter
I stand no chance with all I have
Until your Glory shone upon me
Now I can confidently say
Only You can lift a life.

I desire to please You with all I am
Dormant gifts could not achieve
Until your breath came upon me
Now I can confidently say
Only You can make alive.

ONLY YOU

Prayer (Only You)

Loving God, I acknowledge I am nothing without you. I put my trust in none other than you because only you can satisfy, only you can make me alive, only you can lift a man, only you can change a life. You are all knowing and all faithful God. Holy Spirit, empower me to remain firmly grounded in God and unwavering in my trust in Him. I surrender my all to you, only you are my God, my Lord and my King. Amen.

REFLECTION NOTE TO SELF

Who do you put your unwavering trust in?

35

FOR ME

You pulled me out of the marred clay
With your outstretched hand you rescued me
When all help seemed far from me
Your profound mercy, cried out for me.

You called me out from a place of death
With your mighty power you broke the chain
When the grip of hell held me bound
Your amazing grace, made way for me.

You brought me out from sin and death
With your sacrifice you paid the price for me
When my portion was eternal separation from you
Your everlasting love, made room for me.

You took away my guilt and shame
With your forgiveness you removed the stain
When what I want to do is hide from you
Your loving kindness, called out for me.

You pulled me out of misery and defeat
With your rod and staff you comforted me
When the enemy carefully planned my fall
Your righteous judgement, spoke for me.

FOR ME

Prayer (For me)

My redeemer, I worship you. Everything about you speaks of the depth of your love for me. Thank you for the sacrifice which paid for my redemption. Thank you, Lord Jesus, for paying the price in full. You bore my pain, shame, and you broke every chain of bondage, and I am now free. Thank you for your mercy, your grace and loving kindness, in Jesus' name, Amen.

REFLECTION NOTE TO SELF

How much do you know about what is available for you in God?

SET YOUR EYES ON THINGS ABOVE

Set your eyes on things above
You are alive for a good reason
Circumstances may speak lies
Your experiences may tell a different story
The truth you know will lead you to glory

36

HIGHER THAN I

Lead me to the rock that is higher than I
When the earth beneath me trembles and shakes
May I be confident in your sustaining grace
To remain and bloom where I am planted.

Take me to the place that is higher than I
When life becomes dark and I lose sight of light
May I remember I am seated in heavenly places
To have advantage over circumstances of life.

Fill me with the knowledge that is higher than I
When I feel bound and no freedom in sight
May what you teach me open up the portal of light
To make a way for me and direct my path.

Embrace me with the love that is higher than I
When I feel alone and question my worth
May your sacrifice speak volumes to me
To make me experience a true Father's heart.

Your love is vast and reaches to the heavens
Your cross so big it took it all for me
To know you more,
Is to be on a ground that is higher than I.

HIGHER THAN I

Prayer (Higher Than I)

Gracious God, I worship you. Thank you for being so good to me. I may not always understand what you are doing, but I can be rest assured to trust what you are doing. You are my God, my Redeemer, my Lord and my King. Take me to a place that is higher than I, so that I can see and understand things from your perspective, in Jesus' name, Amen.

REFLECTION NOTE TO SELF

What needs to change for you to see things from a different perspective?

37

FIRE IN MY SOUL

I feel the fire in my soul
The depth in my belly forever roars
I need your grace to hear your groan
That I may fully express your will.

I hear angels singing
The echoes of worship forever rings
I need a heart open and alive
That I may receive life from your throne.

I see the blood that was shed for me
Every stripe on him brought healing to me
I need to receive the sacrifice
That I may stand blameless before you.

I touch your grace at the mercy seat
The works of flesh have no room to stand
I need your fire to purify me
That I may come alive for sure.

I taste your goodness in my life
I am a walking testimony
I need a spirit aligned to yours
That I may be yours through and through.

There is the life of God in me
The spirit of truth abides in me
 Draw me near and draw me close
Let there be a fire in my soul.

Prayer (Fire in my Soul)

Lord of Power and Grace, I acknowledge your goodness and your faithfulness in my life. I am a walking testimony. Help me to never lose sight of your sacrifice of love and help me to see your love expressed to me in diverse ways. Holy Spirit, help me remain surrendered to you. Let my heart yearn for you and my soul be on fire for you; in Jesus' name, Amen.

REFLECTION NOTE TO SELF

What needs to happen for your soul to be transformed?

38

MORE THAN ENOUGH

What else could I ever need?
When the Creator is all for me
All I need to do is look around me
Then, I can confidently ask for anything
You are more than enough for me.

How much peace could I ever need?
When the Prince of Peace is there for me
All I need to do is call out to him
Then, can my understanding be surpassed
You are more than enough for me.

How much joy could I ever need?
When His presence is available to me
All I need to do is come before Him
Then, I can have fullness of life
You are more than enough for me.

How much love could I ever need?
When he gave His all for me
All I need to do is come before Him
Then, I can draw from the everlasting
You are more than enough for me.

For as long as I abide in You
I will not lack any good thing
I will not weep over all thing
I will not strive to have everything
You are more than enough for me.

MORE THAN ENOUGH FOR ME

Prayer (More than Enough)

King of Glory, my Redeemer I worship You. You are El Shaddai, the God of more than enough. You are everything to me and I could never ask for more. I am blessed because my life is secure in you, my hope is sustained in you and my future is assured in you. Empower me by your spirit to look only to you as my source, in Jesus' name, Amen.

REFLECTION NOTE TO SELF

What is your source for more than enough?

39

SMELL THE ROSES

If you can smell the roses
You can taste His faithfulness
Every creature He made perfect
That's all you need to know.

If you can smell the roses
You can feel His gentle touch
Every moment He is near
His essence is all around you.

If you can smell the roses
You can see His loving kindness
Every person He puts around you
Can tell you something about Him.

If you can smell the roses
You can hear His still small voice
Every time you decide to listen
His mind is poured out to yours

May I always
Smell the roses
Taste His faithfulness
Feel His gentle touch
See His loving kindness; and
Hear His still small voice
O Lord, help me to smell, taste, touch, see;
And hear You for all eternity.

SMELL THE ROSES

Prayer (Smell the Roses)

Creator of All Things, I magnify your Holy Name. All creation describes your magnificence and character. Help me to see your beauty and your greatness in everything that You created. Help me not to take anything for granted. Open my eyes to see the mysteries hidden in creation and the intelligence that put all things together. Help me to pause and smell the roses, Amen.

REFLECTION NOTE TO SELF

What will it take for you to stop and smell the roses?

40

ETERNITY

You place eternity within me
Nothing else can fill the void
Your Spirit transforms my spirit
Your life in me is fulfilling
To know you, is for all eternity.

Heaven and earth collide within me
Kingdom come, your will be done
Your power enabled my spirit
Your mind for me is intriguing
To know you, is for all eternity.

Two laws are at work within me
Life and death are the options
Your Spirit quickens my spirit
Your righteousness is redeeming
To know you, is for all eternity.

Purpose is at work within me
Night and day do the bidding
Your spirit equips my spirit
Your glory calls forth the season
To know you, is for all eternity.

ETERNITY

Prayer (Eternity)

Eternal Rock of Ages, I adore you. I stand in awe of your majesty. From age to age you remain the same. Help me to recognise how much you placed inside of me. Let your Kingdom come and your will be done in my life. Thank you, that your spirit makes me alive and helps me to remain connected to you for all eternity, in Jesus' name, Amen.

REFLECTION NOTE TO SELF

How much do you know about God, and what impact does it have on your life?

41

WHEN I DON'T KNOW

When I don't know what to do
Help me to know to wait on you
The wisdom from you is all I need; and
Everything becomes clear to me.

When I don't know what to say
Help me to let you speak through me
A revelation from you is all I need; and
My mouth will utter words of life.

When I don't know where to go
Help me to find my way to you
An encounter with you is all I need; and
My feet shall go and possess the land.

When I don't know what to think
Help me to open my mind to you
The word of truth is all I need; and
My thoughts will be on things from above.

When I don't know how to feel
Help me to give my emotions to you
A touch from you is all I need; and
My heart will flow with peace and joy.

When I don't know why to live
Help me to look to the author of life
A breath from you is all I need; and
Purpose will be birthed afresh in me.

WHEN I DON'T KNOW

Prayer (When I don't know)

Mighty God, you are the source of all my needs. When I don't know what to do, what to say, what to think, where to go, how to feel or why to live; lead me home to you my ever-present help in time of need. Remind me of all the times you have come through for me. Let your wisdom and word illuminate my mind, refresh my heart and direct my path, in Jesus' name, Amen.

REFLECTION NOTE TO SELF

Who do you turn to when you don't know?

42

LIGHT AND DARKNESS

Light and darkness, who can comprehend
Day and night exchange in sequence
When light pierces through the darkness of my eyes
My understanding becomes enlightened.

Darkness disappears at the appearance of light
By your light I walk boldly through the dark
When deep things are uncovered out of darkness
The shadow of death will be brought into light.

Who can hide in the presence of light?
Darkness must give way at the sight of light
When your light shines upon my head
By your light I walk through any darkness.

You spoke, let there be light and there was light
Darkness could not comprehend the light
When I fall and I sit in darkness
The Lord will be a light to me.

LIGHT AND DARKNESS

Prayer (Light and Darkness)

Thank you, Heavenly Father, for who you are and all you have done for me. You are the author of life. You are the bright and shining light; and the Father of all Light. Lord, I pray that your light will illuminate my heart, my mind and my path. Lead me into all truth and guide me by your light. Let every darkness depart at the sight of your light, in Jesus' name, Amen.

REFLECTION NOTE TO SELF

What would having illumination about what to do in an area of struggle mean for you?

43

I GO WITH YOU

When the pressure of life tried to hold me down
My soul is tricked to follow in line
Then, a still small voice whispers to me
Fare on my child, am here with you.

When the tongues of men seek to tear me down
My heart is ripped to pieces unknown
Then, I hear the sound of comfort say
Worry not my child, I call you blessed.

When habits of old rage hard at me
My will oscillates between mine and yours
Then, I feel your grace overshadow me
Stand firm my child, you're justified.

When storms and mountains stare at me
My mind is weary of what may ensue
Then, I am directed to fix my eyes on you
Look up my child, I am here for you.

When I take step towards what you show me
Fear of the unknown lures me to hold back
Then, I am reminded you will never leave me
Take courage my child, I go with you.

I GO WITH YOU

Prayer (I go with you)

Lord, I thank you for who You are. I am incredibly grateful that You are always with me. Thank you for your still small voice that always guides me; thank you for your grace that keeps me going; thank you for providing comfort when I need it most. Thank you for your reassurance that You never leave me, and You always go with me wherever you send me. Dear Holy Spirit, I ask that you help me and empower me to fix my eyes on You when the going gets tough, in Jesus' name, Amen.

REFLECTION NOTE TO SELF

Where would you dare to go if you know God is with you?

HOLD ON TO THE WORD OF GOD

Hold on to the word of God
It holds the keys to your victory
The more you take in
The more you can bring out
To fight and win your battles

UNLEAS<u>**H**</u>

44

STAND AGAINST

Who said it can't be done?
Who said there is no hope for me?
That counsel is not from God
I stand against it with his word
It can be done and there is hope for me.

What obstacle is in my way?
What barrier will stop me?
These strategies will not work
I stand against them in his name
No obstacle or barrier will stop me.

Who is gathering against me?
Who is conspiring for my fall?
Their intention is unjust
I stand against them in His might
Gathering and conspiracy will not stand against me.

Who thought I will not rise?
Who thought there is no victory for me?
That thinking is so flawed
I stand against it with his blood
I will rise and there is victory for me.

I stand against limitations
I stand against barriers in my way
I stand against ungodly counsel
I stand against every lying tongue
Only God's will is permitted to stand.

STAND AGAINST

Prayer (Stand Against)

Lord, I thank you for who you are. I am grateful for your word, your name, your blood and your might that I can always rely on. I stand against everything that is contrary to what you say about me and what you made available for me. Nothing shall be too hard or impossible for me because of you. I can do all things because you give me strength. You are all I need and all I want. I desire to love and worship you all the days of my life, in Jesus' name, Amen.

REFLECTION NOTE TO SELF

What do you need to stand against in your life?

45

READY

When you say it is time, the universe falls in line
Angels are at attention for your orders
Your blueprint offers instructions
Heaven waits for me with excitement
Only may I be ready.

When the Lord of Hosts arises, the chariots falls in line
The enemies forever scattered
The armour of God to the rescue
My words of declaration are effective
Only if I am ready.

When the Father issues commands, the Son and Spirit fall in line
The world waits for his redemption
His blood, the price of atonement
My acceptance activates the power
Only when I am ready.

When I align my will to yours, my destiny falls in line
Your plan is a hope and a future
Daily consecration and sacrifice required
Complete surrender is my lifeline
O yes, I am ready.

READY

Prayer (Ready)

O, Lord, You are worthy of every praise and honour I could ever give. I recognise and acknowledge that I exist because of You. You are all powerful and by your supreme will, You created all things. You also gave me a will to choose. You will never force me to receive what you have for me; You always wait until I am ready. I ask that You give me the wisdom and the discernment to know and be ready at the right times, in Jesus' name, Amen.

REFLECTION NOTE TO SELF

How prepared and ready are you to step into opportunities presented to you?

46

I WILL ARISE

I declare, I will arise!

The ground is not my place
I journey there for perspective
When I have learnt the lessons,
and become the person
It is time to rise up again.

I can't remain defeated
Challenges are meant to be overcome
When I walk through, and grow too
It is time to rise up again.

Failure is not my destination
There are valuable lessons in failing
When I capture the wisdom,
and understand the process
It is time to rise up again.

Disappointment is no good for company
Expectations can sometimes not be met
When you have grieved and accepted your losses.
It is time to rise up again.

Discouragement will keep you small
Don't dwell too much on what is gone
When you have identified your shortfall,
and prepared your come back
It is time to rise up again.

Fear of anything will hold you back
Don't give in to it's many lures
When you have taken back your power,
and get back your sound mind
It is time to rise up again.

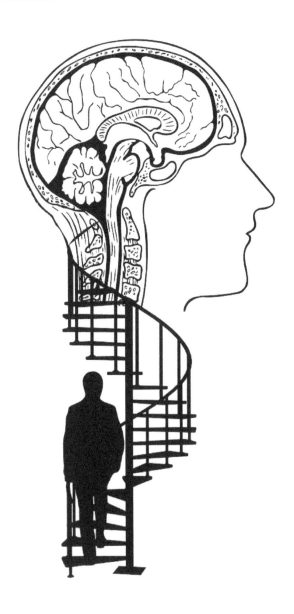

I WILL ARISE

Prayer (I will arise)

Lord, I decree according to your word that I will arise. Though I fall seven times, I will rise up again. Thank you for the wisdom, strength, courage and determination that I developed through failing and falling; thank you for the same that helps me rise up again. Amen.

REFLECTION NOTE TO SELF

What would be different for you if you decide to arise?

47

WHISPER

In the quiet of the night
Your whisper brings the sound
All I have to hear is your voice
And all shall be well by your word.

In the raging of the storm
Your whisper brings the calm
All I have to know is your peace
And all shall be well by your command.

In the midst of dead works
Your whisper brings the life
All I have to feel is your breath
And all shall be well by your touch.

In the absence of vision
Your whisper brings the light
All I need to have is your revelation
And all shall be well by your guide.

In the face of unbelief
Your whisper stirs faith in me
All I have to hear is your word
And all shall be well by your grace.

WHISPER

Prayer (Whisper)

Father, in the name of Jesus, I glorify your holy name. Thank you for speaking to me in different ways. Open my ears to hear your still small voice and the answers wrapped up in your gentle whisper. Let me not be distracted and let me not miss out on every good thing you have in store for me, Amen.

REFLECTION NOTE TO SELF

How much are you missing out on, from the message of the whisper?

48

THE MOMENT

The moment I pray
Answers are dispatched
War in the heavens may rage
Answers will surely come in time.

The moment I go
Provision is already made
Though the journey may be long
You started with the end in mind.

The moment I choose
Power flows in my way
On whose side I am is crucial
Your Kingdom come and will be done.

The moment I fall
Help is sent my way
Even though I may feel defeated
I'm more than a conqueror because of you.

The moment I arise
Destiny comes alive
Divine alignment in action
Your purpose fulfilled in due course.

THE MOMENT

Prayer (The moment)

Lord, you are the creator of time who does not exist in time and is not limited by time. Help me to recognise significant moments and the power they hold to make a difference. Give me the wisdom to understand what to do at opportune moments. Give me the courage to do what needs to be done in the right moment. Empower me to stand firm and give me the strength to go through difficult moments, in Jesus' name, Amen.

REFLECTION NOTE TO SELF

How ready are you to step into your opportune moments?

49

COME FORTH

I call you out of obscurity
You have too much to be hidden
I remove the veil and open the gate
Now, come forth in my name.

I tell dry bones to come to life
You can still march again
I strengthen your heart and guard your loins
Now, come forth in my name.

I ask fountains to flow again
The treasure in you must come to life
I dig new wells and clear the path
Now, come forth in my name.

I command fear to lose its hold
Boldness and power are there for you
I break the shackles that hold you bound
Now, come forth in my name.

I declare abundance over you
Lack has no place to stay with you
My storehouse is open to meet your needs
Now, come forth in my name.

I come forth, out of obscurity
Dry bones come to life again
Fountains are flowing with treasure
Fear lost its hold on me
Abundance is my testimony.

COME FORTH

Prayer (Come Forth)

Lord Jesus, I thank you because you are the very word of God; and God's word will not go back to him void until it has accomplished what it is sent for. Thank you for your word that speaks good things to every aspect of my life. Thank you for your life-giving word. Let your word work in my life. At your word, I will come forth from everything you called me from, in Jesus' name, Amen.

REFLECTION NOTE TO SELF

What needs to happen for you to come forth into the new things God has for you?

50

ROAR

You have been silent for too long
It is time to make declarations again
There is power in your word
Life and death is on your tongue
It is time to ROAR again!

You have been wounded for too long
It is time to rise up again
There is healing in His blood
His balm will mend all the pain
It is time to ROAR again!

You have been exhausted for too long
It is time to stand firm again
There is power to conquer new heights
His word will refresh your soul
It is time to ROAR again!

You have been asleep for too long
It is time to be awake again
There is a new song for you to sing
His strength is available to you
It is time to ROAR again!

You have permitted the enemy for too long
It is time to recover all you have lost
You have the authority to overtake
Goodness and mercy will follow you
It is time to ROAR again!

Awake, awake, sing a new song
Awake, awake, put on God's strength
Awake, awake, decree justice
Rise up and take your place
Rise up, **O**vertake **A**nd **R**ecover
It is time to ROAR again!

ROAR

Prayer (ROAR)

Dear Jesus, you are the lion of the tribe of Judah. When the enemy goes about like a roaring lion seeking to devour me, help me to remember that you are the true lion. By the power in your name and your blood, I close and seal every access the enemy has been granted to my life, knowingly or un-knowingly. I come against and destroy the plan of the en-emy concerning my life. I overtake and recover everything the enemy has stolen from me; and everything he has killed and destroyed in my life. I decree and declare a seven-fold restoration in Jesus' name, Amen.

REFLECTION NOTE TO SELF

What will it take for you to ROAR again?

UNLEASH

Understand there is more for you
Know there are depths still unexplored
There are gifts still wrapped in you
Untapped treasure lay in wait for you
You are more than you currently see.

Never allow the past or present restrain you
The force they exert can overwhelm you
Appreciate the blessings of every season
Remember the change that is set to come
You are not meant to remain stuck.

Let God be your strength
You are not meant to do life alone
When God helps you
Nothing can stop you
Stand in that confidence, you can't go wrong.

Eliminate fear from your life
You have power, love, and sound mind
No more playing small
You have every reason to step up
Destinies are waiting for you.

Align your will to God's will
Submit yourself and draw close to Him
In the fullness of time, His plan will unfold
What is in stock for you will amaze you
Don't give up, keep your hope alive.

Set your eyes on things above
You are alive for a good reason
Circumstances may speak lies
Your experiences may tell a different story
The truth you know will lead you to glory.

Hold on to the word of God
It holds the keys to your victory
The more you take in
The more you can bring out
To fight and win your battles.

REFLECTION NOTE TO SELF

What is the one thing you need to let go of or hold on to, for you to unleash (Break free) and reach out for what is ahead?

THRIVE

I AM NOT OK AND THAT IS OK

I am not ok, and that is ok
I have great days and tough ones too
A listening ear along the way
A burden shared relieves the pain.

Don't look at me funny now
Like you do not have one of those days too
Life can be tough and it takes its toll
Don't judge me, I am human too.

We are not meant to do life alone
Looking out for one another is a priceless gift
If you are close enough to where I am
You will see my pain, no need to hide.

I will not be pressured to be ok all the time
I will honour where I am every moment that pass
Whether you understand is not really the point
Acknowledging my need of grace is the call.

The Grace to withstand the pressures of life
The Grace to conquer when I need to fight
The Grace to let go when it is the best thing to do
The Grace to forgive myself when I fall short
The Grace and courage to ask for help
When I am not ok, that is ok
His Grace will be sufficient for me.

SEX, GOD AND THE DEVIL

What is it about sex?
God and the Devil care about it
The force behind it exceeds the pleasure
It is the strongest binding force that exists
It makes two become one.

Sex is a gateway of exchange
You get more than you bargain for
Soul tied to soul, lives tangled in the tango
The mystery of oneness is attained
It keeps lives connected.

Sex is a pathway to procreation
Seed is planted and life is birthed
The earth is replenished by its product
The law of multiplication is enacted
It brings offspring to existence.

Sex is a weapon in marriage
United as one, against the Devil
Reminder of God's covenant blessing
To love and to honour sincerely
It brings fulfilment to the union.

So what is it about sex?
God wants to preserve it
The devil wants to pervert it
Everyone has opinion about it
Sex is important, we can't deny it.

Register your interest to be notified when the
'NEW VOLUME'
is released.

Prayer of Salvation

Do you know you can have a personal relationship with God through his son Jesus Christ? I am not talking about religion, but asking a question about relationship. God wants to have a relationship with you, His love beckons to you, are you going to answer Him?

If you are ready to start a relationship with God, say the prayer below with sincerity.

Dear heavenly father, I thank you for the gift of life that has sustained me up to this moment. I acknowledge I am still here because you have kept me alive and because you have a plan and a purpose for my life according to Jeremiah 29:11 which says *'For I know the thoughts that I think toward you, saith the Lord, thoughts of peace, and not of evil, to give you an expected end'.*

I thank you for loving me even though I may sometimes not feel it. The bible says in John 3:16 *'For God so loved the world, that he gave his only begotten Son, that whosoever believeth in him should not perish, but have everlasting life'.* I acknowledge my need of you and everything that Jesus Christ did for me on the cross. I accept the gift of salvation and now surrender my life to you. I ask that you come into my heart and be the lord of my life from today. Give me the gift of the Holy Spirit and teach me to know you and walk with you all the days of my life. AMEN.

For more resources to help on your journey, visit: www.queeninsideofyou.org.au and join a bible believing church in your locality.

About the Author

Sumbo Ndi (PhD) is a Nigerian born Australian who is embracing her passion for putting words to her thoughts, insight, and reflection. As a young girl growing up in Nigeria, Sumbo remembers writing her feelings and thoughts in a small notebook and often wrote inspirational words for hand-made cards.

In recent times, Sumbo has been contemplating and reflecting on the intersection of faith and spirituality as it echoes in her daily life and her diverse work experience as a scientist, a coach and counsellor.

Her new book series, Divine Whispers is a collection of uplifting and inspirational poems, thoughts, and prayers. Her writing expresses the hope, faith, love, fears, burdens, dreams, aspirations, and joys of daily living; and the journey of finding meaning and living on purpose. Call it a book of contemplations. Divine Whispers is her outlet for sharing meaning making in her inner world with the outside world.

Sumbo currently resides in Adelaide, South Australia with her husband and children. When she is not writing or working, she enjoys cooking and spending time with her family and friends.

You can connect with Sumbo at www.sumbondi.com.au

Image Credit

Forever Sure: b0red from Pixabay
Wait: OpenClipart-Vectors from Pixabay
Joy: Gordon Johnson from Pixabay
Unstoppable: mohamed Hassan from Pixabay

ELIMINATE FEAR FROM YOUR LIFE
Perfect Love: Gordon Johnson from Pixabay
Weep Not My Child: Piyapong Saydaung from Pixabay
I see: Gerd Altmann from Pixabay
I Wonder: Gordon Johnson from Pixabay
Rest: ???? Cdd20 from Pixabay
I Run To You: OpenClipart-Vectors from Pixabay
You Are: OpenClipart-Vectors from Pixabay

ALIGN YOUR WILL TO GOD'S WILL
In You Alone: OpenClipart-Vectors from Pixabay
Who Am I Without You: SzaboJanos from Pixabay
The Making of a Vessel: StockSnap from Pixabay
I Run My Race: Ponchai nakumpa from Pixabay
Time: James Osborne from Pixabay
Only You: OpenClipart-Vectors from Pixabay
For Me: Vickie McCarty from Pixabay

SET YOUR EYES ON THINGS ABOVE
Higher than I:Clker-Free-Vector-Images from Pixabay
Fire In My Soul: Pete Linforth from Pixabay
More Than Enough For Me: Satheesh Sankaran from Pixabay
Smell the Roses: rsrahul4 from Pixabay
Eternity: by Vicki Nunn from Pixabay
WhenI Don't Know What To Do: Bev from Pixabay
Light and Darkness: Arek Socha from Pixabay
I Go With You: Arek Socha from Pixabay

HOLD ON TO THE WORD OF GOD
Stand Against: John Hain from Pixabay
Ready: Clker-Free-Vector-Images from Pixabay
I Will Arise: Gerd Altmann from Pixabay
Whisper: Rene Jacobs from Pixabay
The Moment: Gerd Altmann from Pixabay
Come Forth: sipa from Pixabay
ROAR: OpenClipart-Vectors from Pixabay
UNLEASH: Jan Alexander from Pixabay

CPSIA information can be obtained
at www.ICGtesting.com
Printed in the USA
BVHW070230171121
621782BV00006B/696

9 780645 275100